Butterflies

Published by Wildlife Education, Ltd.
12233 Thatcher Court, Poway, California 92064
contact us at: 1-800-477-5034
e-mail at: animals@zoobooks.com
visit us at: www.zoobooks.com

ISBN 0-937934-76-3

Butterflies

Series Created by
John Bonnett Wexo

Written by
Beth Wagner Brust

Zoological Consultant
Charles R. Schroeder, D.V.M.
Director Emeritus
San Diego Zoo and San Diego Wild Animal Park

Scientific Consultants
Dan Lindsley, Ph.D.

Bob Brock
Zoological Society of San Diego

Contents

Butterflies play an important role in our world. Everyone knows how beautiful butterflies can be. But many people do not realize that they do much more than simply make the world a prettier place.

For one thing, butterflies carry pollen from plant to plant. This helps fruits, vegetables, and flowers produce new seeds, which in turn become new plants. Also, butterflies and caterpillars—the *larval* or immature stage of what will become a butterfly—are at the bottom of the food chain. This means that they provide food for many other types of animals.

The word "butterfly" was probably first used to describe a common European butterfly, the yellow brimstone. At first, people called it the "butter-colored fly." Then they shortened the name to "butterfly."

Scientists group butterflies and moths in the category, or *order*, known as Lepidoptera, which means "scaled wings." This name fits butterflies and moths very well, because their wings are covered with tiny scales. These are the only insects that have scales.

Butterflies can be found in all but the hottest and coldest parts of the world. More butterflies live in the tropics than anywhere else. That's because in the tropics, there are always plenty of plants for the caterpillars to eat and many blossoms to produce nectar for the butterflies. Tropical butterflies also live the longest—some for up to one year. Butterflies that live in more temperate climates have an average life-span of just a few weeks or a few months. Some live a mere few hours.

Butterflies have always fascinated people. In the 1800s, butterfly collecting was a popular pastime. People hunted, collected, and studied any specimens they could find. Today, many people "hunt" butterflies with cameras so they can "capture" them on film instead of catching them.

Some people plant special gardens with flowers and grasses that will attract butterflies. That's a great way to enjoy butterflies in your own backyard!

WESTERN TIGER SWALLOWTAIL BUTTERFLY

Twenty thousand species of butterflies brighten the world. As you can see, butterflies have a wonderful variety of colors, wing shapes, and sizes. The largest is the *Queen Alexandra birdwing*. It has a bigger wingspan than many birds. The world's smallest butterfly, the *small blue*, measures less than an inch from wingtip to wingtip.

No two butterflies of the same species are exactly alike. Each is a bit different from the other. Often, the most colorful butterflies are males. Females tend to be duller looking, which lets them blend in with their surroundings. This helps to protect them from predators while laying their eggs. But whether male or female, large or small, the fluttering and soaring butterflies make fields, forests, and mountainsides come alive!

CRACKER BUTTERFLY
Hamadryas chloe
(South and Central America)

GOLD-SPOT SKIPPER
Aguna asander
(North America)

NORTH AMERICAN
TIGER SWALLOWTAIL
Papilio glaucus
(North America)

CABBAGE BUTTERFLY
Artogeia rapae
(North America)

PEACOCK BUTTERFLY
Inachis io
(Europe)

TREE NYMPH
Idea leuconoe
(Southeast Asia)

QUEEN ALEXANDRA BIRDWING (MALE)
Ornithoptera alexandrae
(New Guinea)

COMMON BLUEBOTTLE
Graphium sarpedon
(Australia to India)

DOG FACE BUTTERFLY
Zerene cesonia
(Southwestern United States)

AUSTRALIAN REGENT SKIPPER
Euschemon rafflesia
(Australia)

PAINTED LADY
Vanessa cardui
(North and South America,
Europe, Africa, Asia, and
Australia)

GREAT NORTHERN SULPHER
Colias gigantea
(Arctic North America)

BLOOD-RED CYMOTHOE
Cymothoe sangaris
(Africa)

CITRUS SWALLOWTAIL
Papilio demodocus
(Africa)

QUEEN ALEXANDRA BIRDWING (FEMALE)
Ornithoptera alexandrae
(New Guinea)

The largest butterfly in the
world is the female *Queen
Alexandra birdwing*, with
a wingspan of 11 inches.
The world's smallest butterfly
in probably the *small blue*. It is so tiny
that it could fit on the tip of your nose!

SMALL BLUE
Philotiella speciosa
(Asia and Europe)

*L*ike magic, a butterfly changes from a sluggish caterpillar into a beautiful, graceful adult. This magic of nature is called *metamorphosis*. The reason it seems like magic is because the immature or larval stage in this development—the caterpillar—is completely unlike the adult butterfly. Looks, life-styles, and eating habits are different.

There are four stages in a butterfly's life cycle. The first is the *egg* laid by the female. After 5 to 10 days, a tiny *caterpillar* hatches from the egg. The caterpillar begins an eating binge that continues through its stage in a butterfly's life. The well-fed caterpillar now sustains life through the next stage of development— the *pupa* or *chrysalis*. During this dormant but transitional stage, no food is taken in. At the end of this stage, transformation is complete, and the *adult butterfly* emerges from the chrysalis. If conditions are unfavorable at any stage, development may be delayed until conditions improve.

1 A female butterfly knows where to lay her eggs so that the caterpillars will have plenty of the right kinds of leaves to eat when they hatch. A caterpillar would rather starve than eat the wrong plant!

Butterfly eggs, like the ones above, come in many shapes and textures. Some are smooth, while others have grooves on the surface.

2 After several days, the egg is ready to hatch. Then the caterpillar eats its way out of the egg, head first.

Caterpillars are eating machines. They have massive jaws for munching leaves. In their short lifetime, they may eat as much as *20 times their weight in food.*

3 Once free of the egg, the caterpillar turns and eats its shell. The eggshell provides important nutrients that the caterpillar will need to keep growing.

5 Before shedding its skin for the last time, the caterpillar attaches itself to a stem by spinning a silk "button." Once secure, it wiggles out of its old skin to expose a tough new skin. This new skin hardens almost immediately—it is called a *chrysalis*.

4 A caterpillar's skin cannot stretch as it grows. So, like snakes, caterpillars must shed their skins to make room for their bigger bodies.

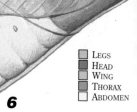

6

	Legs
	Head
	Wing
	Thorax
	Abdomen

Inside the chrysalis, the caterpillar's eyes, legs, and body are broken down into a thick liquid. Slowly, the parts of the adult butterfly begin to form. This process may take days, weeks, or even months. Can you make out the parts of the developing butterfly in the chrysalis above?

Once outside the chrysalis, the butterfly pumps fluid from its body to its wings to inflate them. These fluids must flow quickly, or the wings will harden before they have reached their full size.

8

7

When the butterfly is ready to emerge, it splits open the chrysalis by pumping fluids from its abdomen into its head and upper body. It then crawls out legs first, and turns around to cling to its shell. Its crumpled wings hang downward so that they can unfold more easily.

9

It usually takes a couple of hours for the butterfly's wings to dry and harden in their correct shape. Then the butterfly can fly away in search of its first meal.

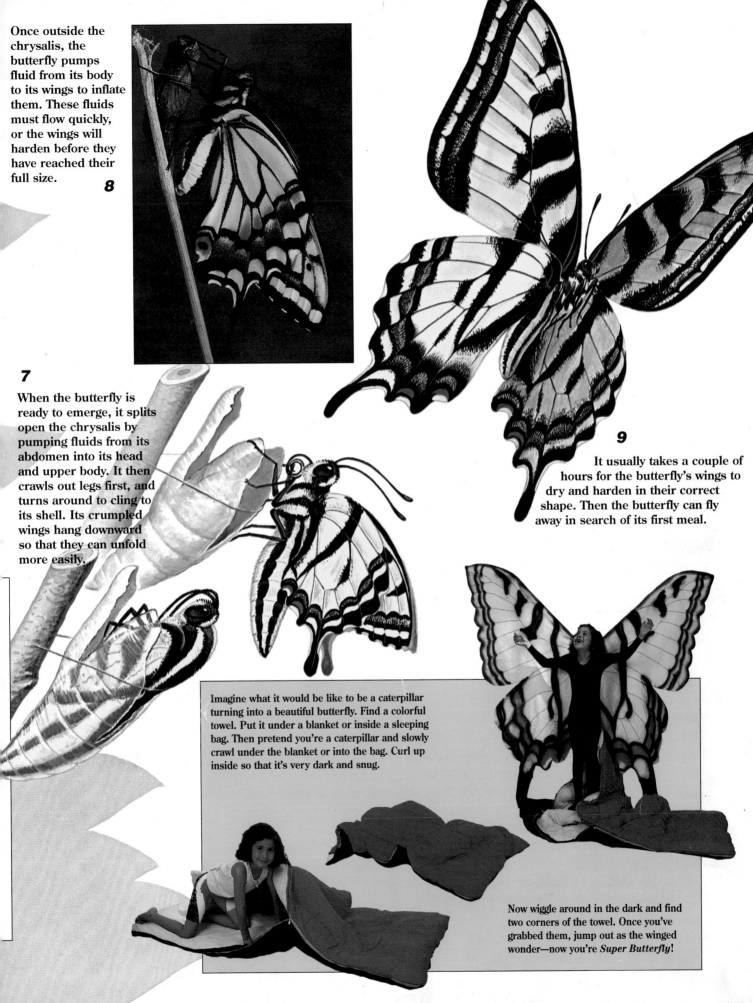

Imagine what it would be like to be a caterpillar turning into a beautiful butterfly. Find a colorful towel. Put it under a blanket or inside a sleeping bag. Then pretend you're a caterpillar and slowly crawl under the blanket or into the bag. Curl up inside so that it's very dark and snug.

Now wiggle around in the dark and find two corners of the towel. Once you've grabbed them, jump out as the winged wonder—now you're *Super Butterfly*!

11

A butterfly's structure may seem unusual, but it makes perfect sense for the butterfly. Butterflies taste with their feet, smell with their antennae, and carry their own straws for sipping nectar!

The most noticeable thing about a butterfly is its striking color. The tiny scales that cover a butterfly's wings give it color and iridescence. Colors serve many purposes in a butterfly's life. They can attract a mate, warn off a predator, and help the butterfly blend in with its surroundings.

A butterfly's body has three sections. Its *head* carries the coiled drinking tube and several sensory devices for selecting food sources, providing balance, a sense of smell, and orientation during flight. Its *thorax* anchors the butterfly's four wings and the six legs that walk and cling. (The feet carry sense organs for taste.) Its *abdomen* holds scent glands and reproductive organs.

Here is a close-up view of a butterfly's scales. You can see how they overlap like shingles on a roof. Underneath the scales, butterfly wings are clear and thin like cellophane.

The moth is the butterfly's closest relative. Here are a few simple ways to tell moths and butterflies apart.

Moth antennae come in all shapes and sizes. Some are ordinary, but many are feathered and fringed. Because moths are active at night, they need extra–sensitive antennae for locating food and mates. Butterflies have simpler, knobbed antennae. But butterflies are active in the daytime and can also rely on sight.

Most moths have fatter bodies than butterflies do. And they are usually much less colorful.

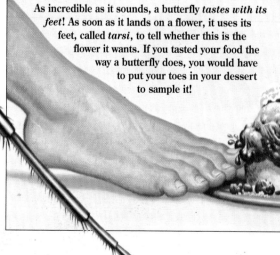

As incredible as it sounds, a butterfly *tastes with its feet*! As soon as it lands on a flower, it uses its feet, called *tarsi*, to tell whether this is the flower it wants. If you tasted your food the way a butterfly does, you would have to put your toes in your dessert to sample it!

A butterfly's skeleton is on the *outside* of its body, instead of on the inside like yours. It is called an *exoskeleton*. It provides the insect with a hard, protective covering for its soft insides.

Have you ever seen a butterfly resting on the ground with its wings wide open? It's soaking up the sun's heat. Butterflies are cold-blooded animals and need to warm themselves in the sunshine before they can fly away.

Although butterflies cannot fly as fast as birds, they use their wings in the same way to flutter, glide, and soar. And the fastest insects, including some of the tropical butterflies, can maintain a flying speed of 24 miles per hour.

Butterflies smell with their antennae to find nectar. Females locate plants where they deposit their eggs. And males use their antennae to detect the scent of females for mating. A special organ at the base of the antennae helps butterflies to orient themselves during flight.

To sip nectar, butterflies have a long hollow tube called a *proboscis*. This lets them probe deep into flowers to reach the nectar. When the proboscis is not being used, it stays coiled up underneath the butterfly's head.

SEE FOR YOURSELF

Would you like to try drinking like a butterfly? First, connect three or four drinking straws so that they become one long straw.

Fill a glass with fruit juice. Put one end of your giant straw into the glass and suck from the other end. Can you imagine drinking all your meals like this?

When a large, brilliant flash of blue flutters through the new world tropics, it is a male *Morpho* butterfly. This dazzling iridescence belongs only to the males—females are a drab brown.

Butterflies and caterpillars are hunted by birds, lizards, monkeys, spiders, and many other animals. But they have some surprising ways to defend themselves and scare away predators. Most butterflies and caterpillars can blend in with their surroundings by looking like bark or leaves. Some resemble bad-tasting insects that predators don't like to eat. And a few are actually poisonous to predators. Predators know which species to avoid and take no chances with an expert mimic.

Other butterflies use their bright colors to startle attackers. Some have spots on their wings that look like giant eyes that might belong to a large animal. This can look scary to a predator. Still others release a bad odor that drives predators away. All in all, butterflies and caterpillars need many ways to escape danger, because predators lurk everywhere and can strike at any time!

The Indian leaf butterfly is a master of disguise. As you can see at left, it is very colorful with its wings open. But when it closes them, below, it looks just like a leaf on a tree.

Birds are the chief predators of butterflies. Because they can attack both in the air and on the ground, birds have more opportunities to catch butterflies than other animals do. So a butterfly that can look like a bigger, scarier bird might avoid being eaten.

The blue *Morpho*, above, flashes its shiny wings at would-be predators. The sudden, shimmering color startles the predator long enough for the butterfly to get away. Some other butterflies also use this *flash coloration*.

16

Some butterflies are mildly poisonous. When a predator eats one, it usually gets sick. After that, it remembers not to eat this kind of butterfly again. It will recognize the butterfly's distinct colors and patterns and avoid it. Poisonous butterflies are only harmful if they are eaten.

A butterfly has an advantage if it looks like a poisonous variety. Over time, some butterfly species have developed into look alikes. This is called *mimicry*. If you were a predator, would you think the moth and butterflies below were safe to eat?

POISONOUS SMOKY WING BUTTERFLY

NONPOISONOUS BUTTERFLIES

NONPOISONOUS MOTH

The hairstreak butterfly can't scare predators away, so it fools them! When threatened, it rubs its hind legs together and makes its trailing tails look like long antennae. Birds and other predators then nip the tails instead of the butterfly's head.

The eyespots on the wings of this owl butterfly from South America look like the eyes of an owl. And when it flaps its wings, the "eyes" look like they're blinking. This can scare away birds and other small animals that are afraid of owls.

Many caterpillars have eyespots on their skin that make them look like snakes. Some swallowtail caterpillars can even rear up at attackers to make themselves look more threatening!

Swallowtail caterpillars have the ultimate secret weapon—a Y-shaped fork in their heads called an *osmeterium*. This fork releases an unpleasant odor that sends predators scrambling. If the smell doesn't frighten them, the bright orange color usually does!

Some caterpillars have patterns that make them look like bird droppings—something no predator wants to eat.

Monarch butterflies travel, or *migrate*, thousands of miles each year. They begin to leave their Canadian breeding grounds in midsummer and by autumn they are in full force, flying south for the winter. In spring, they fly north again.

Many species of butterflies migrate to escape cold weather, but only the monarch butterfly of North America makes a *true* migration, flying south and north again in the same year, every year. Some populations travel as far as 4,000 miles round trip!

What makes this migration even more amazing is that few of the butterflies that begin the journey complete the round trip. Instead, it is a multi-generational relay race! Most of the returning butterflies are offspring that hatched and developed during the southern wintering period. The northbound flight is more grueling. The butterflies set off separately, flying day and night. They seldom rest or eat, but live off their stored fat. Later generations will find their way south the following year—visiting the same places and the same trees that their ancestors have visited year after year. The monarch migration is one of the mysteries of nature.

☐ OUTBOUND
☐ RETURN

Monarchs are well on their way to Florida, California, and Mexico before the autumn chill. Those *east* of the Rocky Mountains and bound for Mexico fly the farthest—more than 2,000 miles. Those *west* of the Rockies migrate about 1,000 miles to the California coast.

ROCKY MOUNTAINS

Eastern monarchs travel in swarms to the plains of Mexico. After several thousand have gathered, they fly high into the mountains. Every year, they stop to rest on the same fir trees.

Some scientists think that migrating monarchs have a built-in compass to point them in the right direction. Others believe that monarchs simply navigate by using the sun. How would you find your way home from a place you had never been before?

Monarchs can migrate to Mexico in two months or less, depending on the weather. Even though they have only a four-inch wingspan, monarchs can travel more than 1,000 miles in just a few days! They coast and glide to save energy, fill up on nectar along the way, and arrive far fatter than when they left!

How can an animal as tiny as a butterfly migrate so many thousands of miles? Scientists have discovered that one way monarchs do this is by hitching rides on winds, storms, and *even hurricanes* heading south! They glide on the wind currents, which carry them more than 7,000 feet above sea level. Airline pilots have reported seeing monarchs as high as 29,000 feet.

The farther south they go, the choosier monarchs become about the winds they ride. They prefer winds that are going toward their southern resting ground.

About *200 million* monarch butterflies spend their winter in a forest near Mexico City. At times, the trees are literally covered with monarchs. But many of these trees are being logged, and the milkweed on which the monarch's larvae feed is being killed. These practices threaten the monarch's future.

Scientists tag monarchs to study them. This is a delicate operation. First, a small area at the top of the wing is gently brushed with the fingertips to clear it of scales. Then a tiny piece of adhesive paper is attached to the wing.

It wasn't until the mid-1970s that scientists discovered where all the millions of eastern monarchs were gathering in Mexico. Scientists now capture, weigh, tag, and release both eastern and western monarchs to learn more about their remarkable migration.

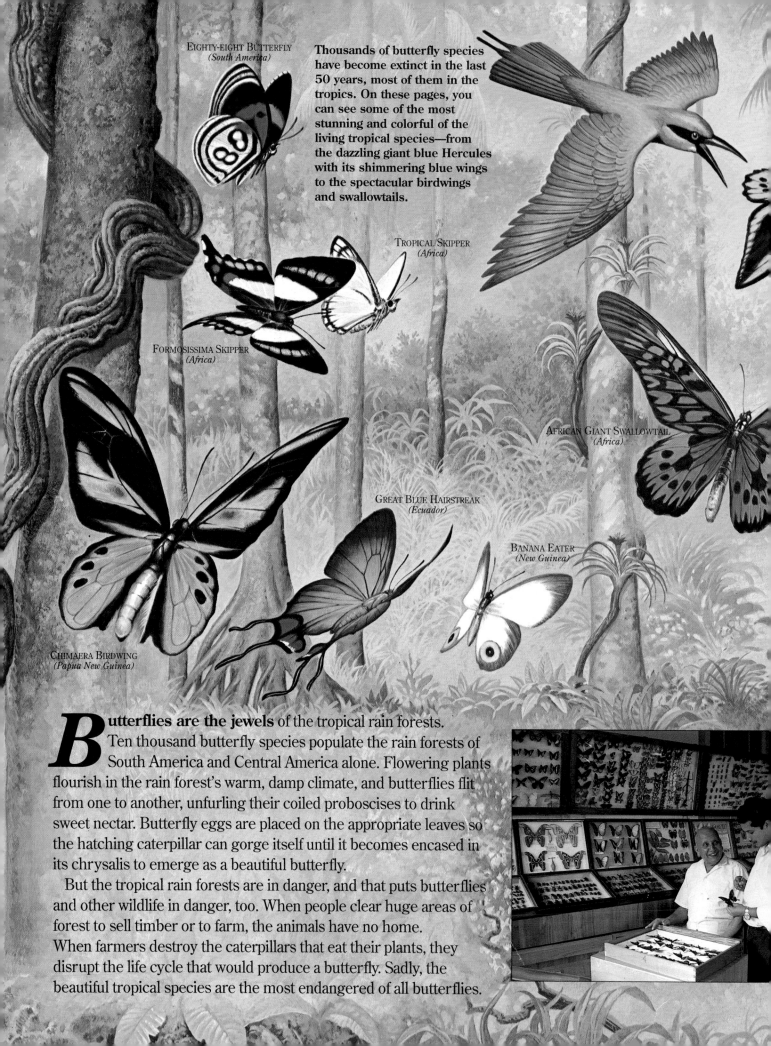

EIGHTY-EIGHT BUTTERFLY
(South America)

Thousands of butterfly species have become extinct in the last 50 years, most of them in the tropics. On these pages, you can see some of the most stunning and colorful of the living tropical species—from the dazzling giant blue Hercules with its shimmering blue wings to the spectacular birdwings and swallowtails.

TROPICAL SKIPPER
(Africa)

FORMOSISSIMA SKIPPER
(Africa)

AFRICAN GIANT SWALLOWTAIL
(Africa)

GREAT BLUE HAIRSTREAK
(Ecuador)

BANANA EATER
(New Guinea)

CHIMAERA BIRDWING
(Papua New Guinea)

Butterflies are the jewels of the tropical rain forests. Ten thousand butterfly species populate the rain forests of South America and Central America alone. Flowering plants flourish in the rain forest's warm, damp climate, and butterflies flit from one to another, unfurling their coiled proboscises to drink sweet nectar. Butterfly eggs are placed on the appropriate leaves so the hatching caterpillar can gorge itself until it becomes encased in its chrysalis to emerge as a beautiful butterfly.

But the tropical rain forests are in danger, and that puts butterflies and other wildlife in danger, too. When people clear huge areas of forest to sell timber or to farm, the animals have no home. When farmers destroy the caterpillars that eat their plants, they disrupt the life cycle that would produce a butterfly. Sadly, the beautiful tropical species are the most endangered of all butterflies.

THOAS SWALLOWTAIL
(South and Central America)

PRIAMUS BIRDWING
(New Guinea)

Every minute, an area of rain forest as large as 40 to 50 football fields disappears. Half of all animal and plant species in the world—*many not yet discovered*—live in the tropical forests. The species destroyed with the forests represent natural medicines and new food sources that we will never know. And many beautiful butterflies will be lost forever.

Some countries, like Taiwan, have made butterfly collecting into a major industry. Although the Taiwanese export 15 million specimens a year, there is no decline in the butterfly population. Why? Because most of the butterflies are collected after they have laid their eggs.

MALAY LACEWING
(Malaysia)

HELICONIUS BUTTERFLY
(South America)

GIANT BLUE HERCULES
(Papua New Guinea)

AGRIAS BUTTERFLY
(Brazil)

HOMERUS SWALLOWTAIL
(Jamaica)

With more than two million specimens, the British Museum of Natural History holds the largest butterfly collection in the world. But smaller butterfly collections, like the one at left, can be found in shops and museums all over the world. Collections such as these help scientists identify and better understand butterflies. And they also help other people learn to care about butterflies.

Brazil, New Guinea, and other tropical countries sell hundreds of millions of butterflies to collectors each year. Fortunately, many of these specimens are raised on butterfly farms instead of being collected from the wild. More and more people are beginning to realize that butterfly farms, like the one above, can help save many species of butterflies.

21

*T*he future of tropical butterflies and other tropical species is linked to the future of the rain forest. While butterfly farms in many parts of the world help to conserve butterflies, they don't do much to save rain-forest habitat. But in Costa Rica, a program called *Proyecto de Mariposas*, or "Butterfly Project," does help the rain forest.

For many years, the villagers of Barra del Colorado, Costa Rica, lived by fishing. Now, there are few fish for them to catch. Commercial fishermen from a neighboring country overfished the area by using large nets called *gill nets* that trap great numbers of fish at one time. With no fish, the people of Barra del Colorado became very poor. Today, they are learning to use some resources of the rain forest in a way that won't deplete them. This is called *sustainable resource* use. It allows people to benefit from nature and encourages them to be its caretakers.

The rain forest of Barra del Colorado was logged 50 to 75 years ago. Its beautiful hardwood was made into furniture and wall paneling for people in other parts of the world. After a rain forest has been cut down, the soil erodes and loses its nutrients. It takes many years for the forest to grow back. Now there is strong regrowth in this rain forest. Villagers are being taught how to make a living from the forest without hurting it. They will farm butterflies to earn money and preserve the forest that is the source of the butterflies.

The *children* of Barra del Colorado convinced their parents that butterflies could improve their lives. A team from the Zoological Society of San Diego suggested *Proyecto de Mariposas* as a science project for the local school, which goes to the fourth grade. First, villagers cleared a garbage dump next to the school for the butterfly farm. Then they planted vegetation that would attract butterflies to lay their eggs and give caterpillars plenty to eat. The butterfly garden and nectar garden will benefit the community instead of enriching just a few.

Soon, the people of Barra del Colorado will be selling their butterflies to exporters in San Jose, the capital of Costa Rica. The children of Barra del Colorado have shown that with projects like these, people can live in harmony with nature.

AFRICAN MONARCH BUTTERFLIES

Index